ARTIST

ASTRONOMER

WORD PLAY!
WRITE YOUR OWN
CRAZY COMICS
#2

CHUCK WHELON

DOVER PUBLICATIONS, INC.
MINEOLA, NEW YORK

NOTE

The comics in this book have tons of clever art, but the speech balloons are empty—it's up to you to fill them! Look at the panels for each comic and figure out the story line, and then come up with the words. Comic scenes involve a corn maze, a fish bowl, Halloween, karate, a monster truck, and many more amusing subjects. You're the writer, and dozens of comic challenges await you.

Copyright

Copyright © 2011 by Dover Publications, Inc.
All rights reserved.

Bibliographical Note

Word Play! Write Your Own Crazy Comics #2 is a new work, first published by Dover Publications, Inc., in 2011.

International Standard Book Number

ISBN-13: 978-0-486-48166-1
ISBN-10: 0-486-48166-2

Manufactured in the United States by LSC Communications
48166205   2017
www.doverpublications.com

BABY CARRIAGE

BALLOONS

BARBERSHOP

6

BICYCLING

CANDY TOWN

CATS

CAVEMAN

CELLPHONE

CINDERELLA

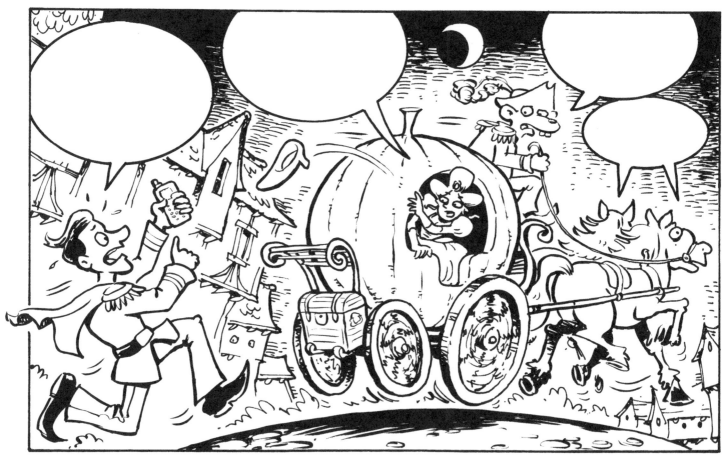

CONSTRUCTION SITE

CORN MAZE

DULL REPORT

FAMILY DINNER

FANCY RESTAURANT

FARMER

FIREHOUSE

FISH BOWL

FISHING

FORTUNE TELLER

GOLF

HALLOWEEN

HIKERS

ICE DANCERS

ICE FISHING

KNITTING

KONG!

LAUNDROMAT

MONSTER TRUCK

OPTOMETRIST

PENGUINS

PICNIC

PIZZA

POP STAR

RAFTING

RAPUNZEL

ROLLER COASTER

SHOPPERS

SOCCER

SPOOKY HOUSE

STILTS

SUPERHERO

TELEPHONE ENGINEER

TENNIS

TRAIN

VENDING MACHINE

VIDEO GAME

VIOLIN RECITAL

WATERWORKS

WISHING WELL

WIZARD

ZOO

MONKEY HOUSE

SLIP